How to Manage Anxiety, Insomnia, and Panic Attacks

While every precaution has been taken in the preparation of this book, the publisher assumes no responsibility for errors or omissions, or for damages resulting from the use of the information contained herein.

HOW TO MANAGE ANXIETY, INSOMNIA, AND PANIC ATTACKS

First edition. February 25, 2023.

Copyright © 2023 Dr. Albert Jhonson.

ISBN: 979-8215289082

Written by Dr. Albert Jhonson.

Table of Contents

Dr. Albert Jhonson

"Nothing is as serious as it seems when you think about it. -**daniel kahnemann**

*The set of techniques at the end of the book

Preface

I know you desperately wish to wake up one day and no longer feel that hell called generalized anxiety. You're tired of all its symptoms and everything it entails. Don't worry, I know exactly how it feels, and fortunately, there is a solution. In this book, I will reveal the methodology that I, as a specialist, use in my mental health clinic ADFER in the United States, and which more than five thousand people have benefited from through this combined system in recent decades. I know there are skeptical people who think there is no solution, perhaps out of ignorance, because they have had bad experiences with treatments, or because they are not familiar with the revolutionary method I employ. In this book, I will show you all the tools that I use as an expert in the field with over 30 years of experience, and that you will execute to finally get out of that nightmare once and for all. And you will see that once you master the techniques, it will be easy to banish the monster of anxiety forever.

"How to Manage Anxiety, Insomnia, and Panic Attacks" is considered one of the best informative clinical books on the treatment of generalized anxiety disorder thanks to the wonderful results in tens of thousands of people around the world. It has been named in the best mental health scientific journals worldwide in 2018-2020.

Author Albert Jhonson, through his personal experience of having suffered from it, tells us from start to finish what it is like to have it and how to get rid of it once and for all. A practical and informative methodology. A step towards your healing.

Enjoy it. Thank you.

About the author

Psychologist, psychoanalyst and psychotherapist from the University of Pennsylvania.

Every time they ask me why I studied different postgraduate courses aimed at mental health; I answer because I suffered from generalized anxiety and all its derivative disorders. I already knew back then that most people would never get out of that dark hole on their own. After I healed, my mission in life was that: to help all those who suffer as I suffered at the time, and I proudly say it; I have been able to help more than five thousand people get out of that dead-end abyss once and for all in my mental health center in New York, and now I put the same system through this book.

Important note

All the information, as well as the methodology and techniques presented in this guide should be taken exclusively as informative material for the person suffering from said disorder. In no way should it be chosen to replace the diagnosis and treatment of a specialist.

Introduction

Who would have thought, that three decades later; I, that patient who is a direct victim of anxiety and all of its symptoms, will find myself on the other side of the road, that's right, helping tens of thousands around the planet to get out of their nightmare: that monster misnamed generalized anxiety disorder. A large percentage of those who suffer from it believe that there is no way out, that the only way is resignation to that hell, but here I am: a survivor, a real chronic case and I verify that this is totally false. Obviously, at the time I believed the same as those people, and that was the reason why I spent many years to find the correct method to get out of that state of mind.

You have no idea how sorry I am for not seeking help, and naturally I let the years go by and my situation became chronic. By human nature we tend to believe that things of this type will be fixed as if by magic, but unfortunately things don't work that way in our reality. When anxiety arrives and takes root in our mind, there are two paths to follow: one, get out of that state or sink into a living hell, until you reach a moment in which you perceive this poor quality of life as normal, but consequently that disorder deprives you of many things that you could have enjoyed and been happy with.

Unfortunately, there are hundreds of millions of people who suffer from this disorder and in the times we live in they have doubled twice. Official data from the WHO estimate that at least 7% of the world population suffers from mild to chronic. And that, obviously, without counting those who have not been diagnosed. Naturally, you don't want to live the rest of your days with that poor quality of life because of that kitty dressed as a monster that doesn't let you be happy. In this synthesized guide I will tell you my real experience of how I lived one of the most severe chronic anxiety disorders to finally find my healing and return to live in peace again.

There is nothing more important in this life than being happy, and that is our mission in this world: to live and enjoy the miracle of existing, of enjoying things. But when an anxiety disorder touches our mind, it makes our whole world collapse, and if nothing is done to banish it, nothing goes back to what it was: it makes us change our personality, it makes us distance ourselves from the family , makes us isolate ourselves from social life, others leave work, many never know love or dare to make their dreams come true, and in particular cases anxiety turns into depression and then comes the worst; they threaten their own life. And that is the heart of the matter, why it is so important to go on time for help and have a personalized treatment, so that it does not evolve to uncontrollable levels and can reach those extremes. Although, it is worth mentioning that only 0.1% evolve to depression and execute what is mentioned above.

When I suffered this suffering myself, I knew absolutely nothing about the tag (generalized anxiety disorder) and much less its disorders that are derived in dozens. They spent almost five years submerged in that hell without having the slightest idea of what he had. Until one day, by accident in everyday life, I came across the famous term, and due to my nature to know a little, I devoured many articles from that time, I'm talking about the late 70s. But as expected, a young adult and Knowing what I suspected of having, everything ended there and I didn't pay any more attention to it, and obviously, my life continued with the same grimace of mental pain that having a tag entails. In the next chapter I will tell you everything, from the beginning to the end with this disease, and then I will expose you the combined system that I manage to be able to heal from it and recover your life that you had before. In those yesterdays I never imagined that I would become a mental health professional, let alone running one of the most important clinics in New York, specialized exclusively against anxiety and its disorders. I have the satisfaction of having been able to help, as I already mentioned, many people with low spirits, and I am completely sure that you will be one more on that list that will say: "anxiety is finally gone." specialized exclusively against anxiety and its disorders. I have the satisfaction of having been able to help, as I already mentioned, many people with low spirits, and I am completely sure that you will be one more on that list that will say: "anxiety is finally gone." specialized exclusively against anxiety and its disorders. I have the satisfaction of having been able to help, as I already mentioned, many people with low spirits, and I am completely sure that you will be one more on that list that will say: "anxiety is finally gone."

Before starting on the subject, I must fervently point out that this guide is not a manual of techniques or miraculous methodologies that are very fashionable today by pseudo health professionals. If you are looking for that, then I must tell you that this book is not for you, because things like that do not work in our reality. Overcoming generalized anxiety and all its disorders are through specific combined steps that we will discuss later. And I know that beyond the system that I manage, techniques, methodologies, to get out of this, is that we have and we must really really want to heal, and that is why as an introduction in the next chapter I wanted to show the way I did it throughout my process. And as you will read in the following pages, you too will have to execute, practice and master this combined methodology until you reach and maintain new mental patterns.

Let's get started. Thank you very much. Dr. Albert Johnson with love. 1948 - present.

One day he came into my life

How could I not remember those winters of 1953 when I was six and completely happy, in my magical world that every little boy creates in his mind. The winters that followed vanished in the blink of an eye and in that time the cruel treatment of my new stepmother took effect in my tender mind where emotions were just beginning to mature into adulthood. Kindergarten, how could I not remember it. Memories still invade me and I feel the feeling of being a child when the first symptoms of the anxiety monster were just appearing. Although, it should be noted that at that time the main problem that showed up was my abused and discarded low self-esteem, trampled by a stepmother. When you are a child and your emotions are just beginning to form, a personality external to you than the one you would have naturally developed takes control in your life and a range of negative emotions begin to show themselves at all times: from fears, thoughts of worthlessness, inferiority, sadness... I still remember when I felt the least of all, I felt I was worthless. And that value that I gave myself was reflected in the way I behaved, resulting in what you would expect from others; weakness in my movements, in the way I behaved and all this was reflected in bullying towards me. Fortunately, as a child, innocence forms part of a shield and protects us from many anxieties, giving us time for moments of joy and happiness.

I remember that because I was self-conscious and had weak self-esteem I was always bullied. How they perceive your body language can be a powerful magnet for those colleagues at school or work to humiliate or respect you. Just evoking that range of feelings still makes my skin crawl. In those years I used to unconsciously wonder why most people preferred to keep bad boys as company? Nobody would hang out with me, in fact, I was a zero to the left and that made me feel worse. I always spent my time alone at recess, or with my bullying partner, another boy who was also bullied, but my self-esteem was so weak that even he hurt me when he was angry because of a beating.

Despite the mistreatment at kindergarten there was no comparison to the humiliation and treatment I experienced at home, where an atmosphere of abuse, threats and beatings of all kinds prevailed, making it a favorable place to develop psychological disorders. When you are a child you tend to overestimate situations, but putting into context what I experienced at home, it was completely realistic. From both father figures I received humiliation and humiliation. I even lost count of the number of times I received hurtful comments from my father that often hit the subconscious harder than a beating, such as: "you are trash, you are good for nothing, you would never have been born a bastard, you are a nuisance, I wish you had died and a long etc.". Even though my emotions in those years were not yet fully mature, they hurt my heart enormously. And not only that, the repeated rapes of my stepmother made everything worse.

I still remember as if it were yesterday the first strange symptom. In my hands and feet I felt the urge to stretch them beyond what was humanly possible, but my compulsive mind told me: "stretch them more and more", and not being able to do it gave me a terrible feeling, added to the tingling sensations, something silly you would think. But self-analyzing myself as an expert of what I experienced, I can undoubtedly say that it was a pre-mental state towards a generalized anxiety that I would later develop.

Not long after that came the obsessive-compulsive disorder (OCD). My parents were a very devout family to a catholic religion, and as expected I was inculcated in it. Around the age of eight I began to have a series of repetitive and irreverent thoughts towards God, which I did not understand at that time, something terrifying to the point of biting and scratching myself to keep them away, because I knew that those thoughts, although unconscious, I recognized that I could read them and that they reached my conscious mind, and the eternal punishment for what the blasphemy represented was present in my mind at all times. They would come regularly at night, I would shake my head trying to push them away, but they would hit my mind over and over again like a short circuit. And even worse when my stepmother would tell me: "you have been a bad animal, you will go to hell when Armageddon comes, etc.".

Time flew... I was a victim of bullying from preschool until I was fourteen. All that time I lived captive inside my own home, I never had friends like any other child, a vital aspect to develop the proper cognitive connections for the optimal development of a healthy emotional state, for the following stages of adulthood. I relate this not to make it longer but to give you an idea of what is to come, and how I developed one of the most chronic generalized anxieties, yet I was able to heal and be happy. I imagine that like you many of those who analyze this guide have not and will not reach my extremes, so have faith that you will be able to get out of this state of mind. And I do not express it with a religious nuance, no! but with the term faith to believe in you, to believe in your ability to achieve your goal: which is to heal once and for all.

Every child and adolescent needs to bond and relate to individuals their own age in order to create - develop the necessary skills that will help them in all facets of adulthood within a society. Therefore, it is critical to develop these skills in order to be relatively successful in our lives. Unfortunately, it was not in my power to develop those skills back then, because I had no friends, no real friendships. Although I always longed for it, but who would want to hang out with someone who gave the impression of a fool, of a weakling, of someone who looked crestfallen and fearful at all times. Such was my self-esteem that at the end of each school day I always left in tears. By the end of high school, social phobia had become my best friend, a disorder that would accompany me for several years in my adult life. I think I am the ideal example of all the active factors that can trigger some degree of generalized anxiety based on traumatic or negative experiences throughout childhood or adolescence, although it also occurs in adulthood.

When you are young it is not at all easy to have an idea of what is going on inside you. In those decades, it didn't even cross my mind that what was making my life hell was generalized anxiety disorder. In fact, I didn't even know the correct term, let alone that day by day without treatment the problem was taking root more and more in my brain. Despite the terrible treatments, in my late teens a fateful event profoundly marked my life. At that time, the death of my father and stepmother in a car accident. Although, they hurt me a lot, not having their "care" and thinking about my future broke me down. By the time I was 17 when I started my working life, it was a horror due to my increased and existing social phobia. Added to a mild compulsive disorder and an incipient anxiety that was just peeking through.

Many people think and believe that social phobia is simply a lack of balls or cowardice, but bah, what could be further from the truth. I can confirm with all its letters that chronic social phobia derives directly from anxiety disorder. And it is not just anything, since it can prevent us from ending all our dreams, from knowing love or having any hope for the future. And it's not enough to put the will and determination into it, no, it goes beyond that. Since the thought that directly feeds the social phobia is an obsessive compulsive thought that is already tattooed in the brain circuits of the social communication area making it difficult only to want to heal, since that circuit is repeated again and again making you afraid to be in social situations, where a large number of people prevail. Every time I went to work in that pasta and cookie factory, a feeling of fear was activated inside me that made me feel weak and feel like going to the bathroom. I was scared to think that something bad would happen to me in front of people, like doing something wrong in the product process and being attacked with hurtful words in front of everyone, and being told that I didn't deserve to be there, that I sucked. The thing is that I felt ridiculed in front of everyone, it was a feeling that just looking into their eyes would be judged, and much worse the looks from the girls would literally terrify me, making me turn red as a tomato and in extreme situations where they would approach me and try to talk to me would make me run to the bathroom to defecate. Although, it should be noted that the main fear of suffering from social phobia goes beyond fearing looks and who it comes from. The main fear that fuels this disorder is criticism, the fear of criticism, of being judged. We are terrified of being attacked, judged and criticized by being watched and fearful of our physical appearance or behavior. I should mention that from my 18th to my 25th birthday I was a failure at every job, I didn't stay long at each one, at most a week or two before I quit. I felt criticized, singled out, although to be honest looking back on it, those were just my assumptions. And that's what the mind of a social phobic with anxiety does, it thinks that everyone criticizes them, that it's the center of attention when it's the furthest thing from the truth.

When suffering from phobia caused by anxiety we think that all the natural looks are critical looks and that they go directly towards us. Even for example when you arrive at a self-service store and a cashier's look falls on us, in our thoughts dozens of things out of reality appear as: "he sees me like that because he thinks I am a robber, he thinks that because of my dress I am annoying and I must buy the product as soon as possible so he thinks that I will really buy and not just look, he likes me, he dislikes me, and a long etc.". You can't imagine the tears I shed from job to job, I felt like shit, a failure, useless... In those years I had no dreams, I just wanted to stay in a job, earn my money and be able to buy food, but I never really succeeded because of the social phobia due to anxiety.

Although I never developed a moderate depression, I did feel down and hopeless because of the bad economic situation that came from all that. There were many years of hunger in my aging aunt's house, and all to avoid wasting her resources because her useless nephew was not able to last more than a week working in the midst of many people. I would go out to look for a job praying not to find one, not out of laziness but because I was terrified of being watched. I still remember that my biggest dream at that time was to have a job where there were no people. The ideal was to work away from everything. A lighthouse would be great, I told myself. Out at sea on a dock, where only the paycheck would arrive every two weeks, but they were only dreams, that yearning never happened. I had no choice but to work one week here, two weeks here, two weeks there, one week here. By the age of 26, I had literally worked all over the city. More than 55 factories.

By that age I already felt like shit, a piece of garbage, there were plenty of adjectives to describe me in those years. By that time suicidal thoughts were swirling in my mind, but I was too scared to do it, I just repeated every day that I would do it, but it was only to somehow minimize my despair and frustration. Just in those years was when my generalized anxiety with all its symptomatology formally began. And it was no longer occasional, but my daily nemesis. By then I thought it had to be stress, but I was wrong. And as expected, I didn't give it the importance despite the fact that it was directly affecting me in all facets of my life. Usually the fear of public exposure generates too much suffering for the sufferer, and that usually we tend to take the easy way out, which is to isolate ourselves, to hide in our bubble; the house. And that is precisely what I did.

Those who suffer from this disorder, do not really know how they project themselves to others when they are observed, but their thoughts assiduously bombard them with questions such as that they are being observed and what they will think of what they see of their physique, and exactly feeling criticized, evaluated and judged at all times is what causes so much fear and discomfort that they reach the point of isolating themselves. "People with low self-esteem and social phobia firmly believe that they are being looked at in a bad way without that really existing, it's all mental and the perception they see in their mind."

As rational and emotional beings, we naturally at some point in our lives long for a partner, it's not always the rule, but almost all of us at some point feel that fire inside us, that urge to desire to be loved by someone outside of our family. I began to feel it in my twenties, I longed to find that special someone, but I must say, it never appeared. It was impossible for me with such disorders to be able to conquer a girl. The few girls that ever made conversation with me in some sporadic jobs I had, their mere presence literally paralyzed me and as expected I bored them, because of my extreme fear I didn't say anything. My mind, my fears, my null social skills were what at some point made me resign myself to never knowing love, due to the terror I felt just imagining to relate with a person in reality, "and if I bore her, if I cannot support her economically, what can I talk about, I would say to myself.

People who suffer from emotional problems of social phobia or generalized anxiety do not usually say so. But that feeling of loneliness and failure that exists, you will not let me lie if you are living it now, is sometimes self-victimizing, that makes us feel very good, it becomes something that calms us, and at the same time hurts us. Things like: "I will be left alone, nobody will love me, I am useless, I am worthless, I wish I would die tonight and not open my eyes tomorrow", all those negative feelings of sadness and frustration and bitterness, somehow it becomes a drug for your subconscious, but you feel good in your bubble, in your fantasy world. Somehow, our mind compensates for that whole range of emotions in moments of resignation to not being able to achieve all our dreams. And it compensates them with depression, sadness, frustrations, and a long etcetera of emotions. And little by little it causes new tag symptoms to emerge, which you didn't know existed before.

For those years, although they directly affected my life, I was somehow able to cope with my social phobia and compulsive obsessive Toc, or negative thoughts. I was able to some extent to cope with those things. But one night something happened that I couldn't cope with, and that's when a nightmare started. Prior to that, I should mention that I had been very stressed out for a few weeks because of all of the above, fearing that I might have a disease or something like that. That night I woke up suddenly, I turned on the light and I felt confused and strange in my body, added to the dizziness, the whole picture was quite new to me. My breathing was accelerated, I tried to catch my breath with every puff, my mouth became dry, accompanied by a little cold and to that I added the furious tachycardia of my heartbeat. I was as scared as I had ever been. I sat on the edge of the mattress, when all of a sudden I felt a terror that what I was experiencing was a heart attack. And so it went on for the next few minutes, until there came a moment when I resigned myself to die. I thought that I would stay there, but then it passed and uncontrollable tremors came literally, everything was shaking, legs, arms, hands, added to the thoughts that told me that I was going to die there. And that only minutes were enough to lie unconscious. And it was those thoughts that made me run out into the street, wake up my aunt and go out screaming like crazy, paranoid, saying that I was going to die. My aunt told me: "stop this nonsense, nephew, it's night to be doing these antics". I got lost at the end of the street, but in the middle of running, the symptoms I felt began to diminish, and I came back very tired, ashamed of that little scene in front of that unknown, and that later I knew as a panic attack. And what months later was the same, they were repeated over and over again. And they are one of those types of symptoms that are almost impossible to endure by willpower. I must say, it is almost impossible to fight a panic attack by mental strength, because it is anxiety unleashed in all its manifestations. And it is in a way, that when a panic attack breaks out our subconscious is giving us an indirect message as if telling us: "help me! get your life in order".

As human beings we are amazing, but those qualities are what make us fragile. Even though you live in chaotic and stressful situations, you are adaptive and almost always learn to live in spite of your environment.

And that is exactly what happened to me. Little by little I was assimilating in my own way all this range of emotional problems, and yes, I learned to live with all that in spite of my terrible quality of life. And I must point out that when I say I learned, it does not mean that you have to resign yourself to live like that. Fortunately, there are systematic methodologies to cope with them. As Buddha said: "if you were born in this plane and you do not dare to make your dreams come true and feel life in all its manifestations, it is better to have stayed in non-existence, in the lights of the cosmos, because if you are born in this life it is to enjoy the experiences and be happy". And beyond channeling it to spiritual issues, Buddha's quote is true, we are on this earth to dare to live every experience without fear of what people will say and unfounded fears. The techniques that I will show later are to do them and not be afraid to execute them, because the reaction of each one is a reward, a little step of the ladder to reach the goal, which is nothing more than being able to control your anxiety, that state of mind that is preventing you from being happy and doing the things you loved before or simply being at peace with yourself and others.

Fear not! I felt worse than you. I know you will be able to come out victorious and look back and exclaim why didn't I do it before? Attitude is a key point in achieving this. I want to point out that if this book at least changes your attitude and your feelings about your anxiety disorder a little bit, it will have accomplished its main goal. Even if the system of techniques didn't work 100% for you, but I know they will, I guarantee it.

When this evil appears and lashes out with all its power it will never stop on its own, and to let it go is only to give it more power to start the day you least expect escalating symptoms one after the other, and that is exactly what happened to me. Once I experienced the panic attacks new ones followed, especially at night: uncontrollable anxieties, irrational fears without foundation that made me go into despair and made me scratch myself until I drew blood to try to calm down, and I succeeded, but causing me a lot of damage. And that is exclusively due to the fact that when we scratch our brain releases an exaggerated amount of hormones of happiness and tranquility. It is not a method I approve of because it becomes a routine and then a habit, which our subconscious learns to endure and then hurt itself, and it is something that will never bring relief. Such harmful habits like smoking or taking drugs to calm the martyrdom of anxiety will never bring relief and peace of mind definitely.

Exactly the symptom of anxiety-induced distress is one of the worst. To mention, in the United States the cases of suicides registered by this symptom are at least 2453 per year. It may not seem very high statistically for a country with more than 300 million; 2 in almost a million, but it is already a focus of attention by the WHO worldwide. What makes it really distressing and worrying is that these attacks usually last more than 40 minutes, and many people in that time can do crazy things, such as commit suicide or throw themselves out of the window.

At that time I did not have enough money to go to a specialist so I learned to live with the condition where there were unbearable periods and others where it decreased a little or insomnia appeared and made me cry for not being able to sleep. In order not to go on for too long, I will mention the symptoms I experienced before starting to look for adequate help, and how I found the exact ways to achieve it. It should be noted that not all symptoms appear all at once. Anxiety is progressive. If you let too much time pass you will experience almost anything depending on whether you have moderate or chronic.

"At 26, I felt like a piece of garbage, just like millions of young people who call themselves that in their loneliness, but before society in their daily lives they try to appear to be strong, when their sad reality is a loneliness full of bitterness and tears for their feelings. Society usually criticizes what they do not know about the background of things, they only look at the superficial without knowing about the emotions at play. How many times I was called and judged as conceited just because I passed by colleagues in the work area without turning to look at them. What they didn't know is that I acted that way out of fear of being stared at, a product of my low self-esteem and social anxiety. Unfortunately, people have zero knowledge of emotions, let alone empathy. As a specialist, a dream that I would love to see come true, if it is not too much to ask, is that all schools in the world would teach subjects on emotions, such as emotional intelligence and all those that stem from it. If only that were done, the world would be a very different place. There would be more empathy and more tolerance. Remember that appearances can be deceiving, just because you see someone happy and smiling does not mean they are happy. There are always undertones to everything.

Below, I summarize a list of the symptoms that anxiety usually presents in each area of our body and how it affects them powerfully. I want to be reiterative and say that I experienced all these symptoms, I suffered them in my own flesh, so I know how you feel, you are not alone. Although it is usually very complicated to explain them in words, but I know the terrible feelings you experience. You will not die, believe me, I assure you!

In our nervous system

We experience: repetitive headaches, memory loss, specifically when there are strong anxiety symptoms, dizziness, sudden changes of character, lack of concentration, tremors, shortness of breath known as dyspnea, tight chest, insomnia, you can not sleep and from this derive others such as terror that the morning comes and you have not slept at all, uncontrollable emotions such as sadness, anger, extreme tiredness, frustration for not being able to achieve your dreams, muscle aches, weakness in arms, tense jaw and tingling in the middle of the face or arms.

In our digestive system you could present: in severe anxious situations you could present diarrhea, colitis in social situations such as job interviews, if you propose to a girl surrounded by people you could have excessive gas (farts), urge to shit, constipation, nausea, choking sensation, dry mouth (Halitosis) etc.

In your cardiovascular system you could have sensations such as: strong tachycardia ranging from 110 beats to 170 beats per minute. Non-focalized burning sensations, i.e., you feel them in the back or front, although not specific, all this is part of anxiety, obviously first rule out any real physiological problem.

In your respiratory system you may experience: a feeling that you cannot expand your lungs and that turns into shortness of breath, an inflammation in the nostrils known as rhinitis, as if they feel clogged, a feeling of tightness in your chest, especially when you lie down at night.

In the skin could present: excessive sweating, tingling, sensation of heat, scratches due to scratches that are produced unconsciously when suffering panic attacks.

Concerning our sexuality we could present: in spite of my youth, in my twenty-five years I was self-satisfied for lack of a partner. In those years I noticed that my erections were weak to the point that they could not become strong and therefore triggered more frustration and anxiety that increased, since sexuality helps somehow to release emotional stress and release energy. My problem became more serious as I felt the genital flaccidity in all its manifestations. Something to mention is that premature ejaculation occurs in severe cases of generalized anxiety, and some people feel a fainting sensation when they are about to ejaculate and everything is a product of the nervous system, it is something little talked about, but it exists, and many even stop having sex because of these sensations of imminent death. So it decreases the quality of life and becomes apart from anxiety in more frustration for not being able to masturbate or have sex. For this reason, it is imperative that general practitioners have the sensitivity to diagnose more than the obvious and get to the bottom of the root cause and refer you to a specialist. This will avoid wasting years and even decades in a lousy quality of life and unhappiness. And beyond that, in order not to waste our life, which we only have one. And getting used to this disorder means that we will never be able to fulfill our dreams in all facets. As specialists, that is our responsibility, that is our Hippocratic oath: "to help and to do everything in our power, if it is in our hands, to return a patient to health by the means of physical and mental science".

By the end of my 26th year, I was battered by a gale of negative emotions and thoughts that assaulted my mind every day. By that time I wanted to kill myself, but my cowardice and survival reflex prevented me from doing so, even though I no longer had anything or anyone to live for according to me. One afternoon while coming from one of those occasional jobs I had, I stopped for a minute at a lottery booth and thought, "if I could win it my problems would go away, I would go to a lonely place with no one to judge me", although, what dreams I had! I know, dreams too immature for my twenty-something years, but all I wanted was to disappear from society, one because of my social phobia and the other because of my generalized anxiety. I always repeated this to myself: "why live? in a couple of years I'll be 30, and at that age there's nothing to live for, if I didn't achieve anything in my 20's, I won't achieve anything in my 30's and something". So I took out my only three dollars that I had and that was the cost of the ticket, so I decided to buy the lottery ticket. And yes, very bad way to spend the money, because I had to walk about 6 kilometers to get home. But by blessed fortune, three weeks later a miracle had happened, I don't know what to call it, I know it sounds like a movie what happened next. In the newspaper section of lottery winners my name appeared, with the title "congratulations to the winners of 5 thousand dollars and the first place Johnson who has won 15 thousand dollars". Reading that was crazy, it seemed like the "gods" had finally taken pity on me. Although to be honest, I am still an atheist.

I knew very well that this amount would not last me forever, at most a year or two. So I immediately thought: "what if I use it to heal myself, whatever I have? It was a question that haunted my mind for several days. A part of me told me: "no, don't do it, it's not worth it, you have nothing, it's part of you to be like that, better spend it on pleasures, go with women and become a man for once, enjoy it". On the other hand, my rational side told me to use it no matter if I spent it all in the process, as it was the only way again to be happy. In the end neither side won the first few weeks, but, at least I started to take an important step in my mentality. By that time I started consuming all kinds of psychology and mental health articles, and that's when I began to learn the terminology of generalized anxiety disorders and their derivatives, and obviously, I was made to suspect that I might have that. But, beyond prompting me to immediately go for help, I continued living my life, until I met Karly, a girl from my neighborhood that even though she did not know of my existence, the part of wanting to be loved was activated in me, and I swore to myself that this girl would one day be my wife, and for that I would have to make a change in my life. To tell the truth, obviously that immature way of acting of wanting to feel loved was just a late impulse of wanting to find a partner. But still, they served as a motivation for me on certain days. Obviously, I must say now that you should never make someone or something push you to want to feel good mentally or physically, but you should want to feel better because you love yourself, the rest comes by inertia.

I went for help to at least five general doctors, and because of the symptoms I described, one of them finally referred me to a mental health professional. Subsequently, this one with a psychotherapist, the most indicated in treating these conditions. I am talking about 1985, and for those years the technical methodologies for anxiety were not scientifically endorsed or advanced as they are today. Likewise, it is worth mentioning that there were several treatments that I carried out, but as expected, without the effectiveness that one would expect. -And so I spent some time without reaching my healing. By that time I only wanted to eliminate my social phobia and my panic attacks, two of the tag symptoms that most prevented me from living in peace. By the time I was in the process of finally finding the right one, a problem came up: insomnia, and it was one of the most distressing symptoms I have ever witnessed in my life, and it did not go away until I executed the combined method we will see below. On the verge of throwing in the towel and sending everything overboard, I found by chance a wonderful person in the Albert Street neighborhood in New York where I lived. And that according to his personal experience he had lived a similar experience to the one I was suffering, and that after taking a combined method he had been healed. It was a person who came at just the right time, the kind that happens one in a million. Despite being shy, I was able to have a pleasant conversation with him and he told me about the methodology he used to heal and who taught it. Obviously, I was not going to miss this opportunity, I thought. Unfortunately, when he told me where this person was located, I thought: "impossible to go". To be honest, I was not entirely convinced at first. How was it possible that in a village in India there was an individual who imparted a methodology for the spirit and soul as he called it to heal. Just to go there would cost me a third of what I had earned. So a few weeks after being undecided and struggling with my demons and imploring that it was not a fraud; I decided, and I did everything to put my documents in order, and I gave an incentive to that good man from India, who obviously would accompany me to obtain my definitive healing according to me.

With all my fears, I had finally arrived with the aforementioned "guru" and teacher. To be honest I was expecting to meet a guy like the typical shamans and their extravagant costumes, but it was totally the opposite. My Hindu friend took me around Bug Gayia Higar a place full of huge mountains and mysticism beyond where the iconic Buddha found his famous enlightenment. When we arrived at the site, a large old wooden house immersed in huge gardens was present. There was not even a glimpse of an office with signs that made me think that this was serious and from a specialist, but nothing of the sort. Neither guru nor Hindu this person appeared to be, he was clearly a westerner who had probably lived most of his life in that place. I should mention that the peace that this man transmitted was evident, and his conversation was pleasant and exquisite. For me, beyond taking advantage of this trip to India to entertain myself and forget my problems a little, I was also concerned about immediately starting any treatment - method that would help me to heal, but it did not happen that way. Fortunately, he gave me free lodging for all the months I needed before he finally decided to help me. I must comment that my Hindu friend Karlek never mentioned in detail the famous methodology with which he claimed to have been cured. Let's just say that he behaved in a strange way as if somehow he was the one in charge of finding the wealthy deranged clients who would accompany him to the other side of the world, desperate to find healing in their lives. By a certain point I thought it had all been a hoax, although at least I thought I had visited the other side of the world, and I was a little de-stressed, although that meant having wasted almost half of the money, but what did it matter, at least a new experience I thought, although the damn anxiety would always chase me everywhere I went, I said to myself in my heart.

- So the cute little kitten is up to his mischief," said the elderly man as he greeted me, and I thought to myself, "he's crazy, damned if I came here just to listen to nonsense from another crazy person.

Immediately after that came a series of dissertations that began to make sense and he started talking about generalized anxiety disorder from A to Z, which obviously left me impressed.

Mr. David Thomson, may he rest in peace and my first mentor, at that time was a specialist in applied psychology, psychotherapy and psychoanalysis, in addition to having various courses and master's degrees. After living most of his life in the United States, he undertook a spiritual year trip to India, and the wonders he saw made him stay in that land. He was 43 at the time, and clearly knew what he was talking about. For obvious reasons, for a moment I thought, "a retired specialist", but did Karlek make me make this trip all the way here to consult a specialist I could have found in my country? Immediately he started talking more and more.

The fact is that Dr. David Thompson had spent much of his professional life around the globe, gathering and creating a unique methodology to help control, heal or get relief from generalized anxiety. And what had driven him to do that was his wife who had passed away as a result of suicide. Specifically after a depression that was directly caused by brutal anxiety just before he became a specialist. And following his example, I too became a psychotherapist. I started a little late to study this wonderful world, and by my 39th birthday I obtained a master's degree in psychotherapy and psychology, in addition to other master's degrees and doctorates. I would like to point out that Dr. David Thompson's combined methodology and his first compilation that he published in 1960 were taken from his book "How to find peace of mind when you have anxiety" which there are only two copies in the world and one is in my possession. Although at the time he was not recognized worldwide for his great contributions, a large number of renowned psychotherapists today use his improved methods based on his work.

After two months and having learned everything from my great mentor Dr. David Thompson, I started with the combined treatment, and after five months I was a new me. I must say that it seemed like a miracle, but of course it was not, but it was thanks to the combined method that proved to be extremely effective in me. And of the techniques. I stayed almost 12 months in India assimilating, learning everything from my great mentor. When I returned to the United States I brought a different mindset with me in order to help those who were in pain as I was. Sadly, my dear friend and mentor lost his life three years later when I was finishing my second doctorate in applied psychology. I am eternally grateful to fate that I met Karlek because without him I would never have met David and thus helped thousands of people around the world. Today that is exclusively my mission in life: to help. Before I start with the techniques to control, alleviate or overcome each of the disorders that derive from the tag, I want to be emphatic that I am now happy. Indeed, I never relapsed again once I was completely healed. The combined method lies in changing the mental pattern towards positive thinking which is in the end what will get you out of anxiety. From there the whole symptom picture is derived, and when it starts to take effect, all those symptoms will disappear.

Today at 68 I feel great that I have been able to help thousands of people to regain their lives. The only way to get back to perceiving and feeling life as it really is. Naturally I always recommend, I urge that, although in this guide I expose the list of the most effective techniques, it is best to carry it out at the same time with face-to-face specialized help, because in that way there will be a 98% of guaranteed healing.

Therefore, you will execute to the letter what I show in this guide based on my experience, but not without first consulting a mental health professional. My goal in this book-audiobook is that all those who read it again regain their happiness and enjoy their life again. Believe me, it is frustrating and a nightmare to lose years, decades of your life imprisoned in your home for fear of what people will say, not having a work life, social life, love life, fear of criticism or any disorder derived from the tag.

Now is the time to go for help and to execute what I will expose here, that way you will get all the tools to be able to enjoy your life again. Enjoy it!

List of combined techniques. Run them three by three every day of the week

I determined that I would not focus on complicated definitions of each disorder because I believe that most people who are looking for a practical solution are probably already aware of what generalized anxiety is and what it entails and its derivative disorders, and what really affects them. What matters is trying to do something different to try to heal. It is for this reason that I will immerse myself fully in the practical methodology. Although, I will expose the main techniques that helped me control it, I will also expose others already known that, if you already know them, will help you within the combined methodology. Before starting I want to be very repetitive and punctual in this: whatever happens, do not let any day go by without doing them, It is essential for the mental patterns that will be the basis of change within your subconscious to be created in your mind and will automatically be projected into your real life. Therefore, even if you feel bad due to panic attacks, insomnia, anxiety and other disorders, continue with your goal in mind. Remember that brick by brick a house is built, and so you with each exercise, new way of thinking, positive routine executed day after day; you will be building a new mentality in the face of different situations that today keep you imprisoned in your mind. Remember, you must be disciplined, and do not be in a hurry, do them without haste, always relaxed, and with a lot of faith. It is essential to truly believe in your new lifestyle, techniques and routines because everything that I expose here works as a whole and they are effective in the majority of my patients. So without adding more let's get started!

Exercises especially against anxiety

Applied Mind Breathing

It serves exclusively to calm anxious states and prevent panic attacks to a greater extent.

The exercise known as applied mental breathing is carried out in this way; you should be lying as comfortable as possible with your head slightly elevated and arms at your sides. 15 minutes you must stay like this. I clarify, it is not meditation exactly because you combine it with mental images. Let's see.

- At this moment you will begin to close your eyes, breathe through your mouth, I want you to take a deep and natural breath... then you will hold it for a maximum of 7 seconds..., then you will begin to expel it in small exhalations, first through your nose and then through your mouth until that you feel your lungs completely empty.

- Again we will do the simple exercise, but this time we will add a mental image of a scenario. When I mention this, I mean any place, a scenario that violates your security-peace and harmony, try not to think too much about the scenario, the important thing here is that your mind takes you to those places or atmospheres, but being aware of reality. To cite an example, take a deep breath through your mouth, then think of a wheat field full of peace at sunset... continue immersed in that landscape... Hold your breath for 7 seconds then make a few small exhalations through nose mouth nose mouth until you expel all the air from your lungs, and again you begin to breathe deeply through your nose and mouth and continue in the same scenario that gives you peace... Take a deep breath, hold 7 seconds, then you remove all the oxygen through your nose, mouth, nose, mouth, until empty. The ideal is 15 minutes, but it can be 10 if you decide. Do not do it fast but with normal breathing. The first is deep, but the others are natural and controlled. Only when you hold the 7 seconds and exhale. This powerful, simple and effective exercise exclusively serves to stop anxiety states and prevent panic attacks. You can do this exercise in the morning or at night before bed. The important thing here is to combine all the exercises that you are mastering to do them with better results.' This powerful, simple and effective exercise exclusively serves to stop anxiety states and prevent panic attacks. You can do this exercise in the morning or at night before bed. The important thing here is to combine all the exercises that you are mastering to do them with better results.' This powerful, simple and effective exercise exclusively serves to stop anxiety states and prevent panic attacks. You can do this exercise in the morning or at night before bed. The important thing here is to combine all the exercises that you are mastering to do them with better results.'

The technique of catching or following your active thoughts

*Remember that the first few times you will practice guiding yourself, then you will learn them by heart.

Close your eyes for 12 minutes. The effectiveness of this exercise is basically that you will concentrate on finding your self, self-calming yourself only by following your thoughts that come out of your mind without giving it importance beyond its duration. Being a simple technique, but effective resides exclusively in decreasing the mental revolutions because you will not be the one who will produce the thoughts as it usually is in anxious people but you will let the thoughts flow automatically from the subconscious mind. If they take you to the future, you will follow them without giving them the importance not to extend them, if they take you to the past the same or to the present. You will do nothing, you will only chase them trying to catch them, but up to there, and you will do it at their speed until they disappear. Try to do this exercise lightly lying down on your bed would be perfect. No more than 12 minutes, with normal breathing. It is immediately the feeling of tranquility due to the brain waves down to levels where relaxation is manifested. You will only be chasing them, you will not extend them longer than they last nor will you question them, you will only observe their beginning and their fading. We know that thoughts are not static and are always active in movement until they disappear, for this reason you will only follow the thought. This technique is very effective to reach mental states of peace immediately, because you only follow a flow of source thoughts, unlike when you focus on them and question yourself, and because of that they arise more and more until they become a stream of secondary subthoughts derived from giving them too much attention. Remember, it is not avoiding them, but not giving them the limelight and making them longer than they would last, and turning it into a mental pattern in the instant and repetitive thoughts that in the end is part of the disorder. So remember, close your eyes, breathe naturally and pursue your thoughts as they arise, do not question them or lengthen them, only as long as they last with the sole purpose of calming your mind and lowering the anxious state.

Technique to calm your thoughts

This simple technique consists of calming your mind by self-calming mental patterns that indirectly or directly generate restlessness, anguish, discomfort, if they are present. But without going beyond forcing yourself. Find the quietest place you feel to do it.

Breathe in as deeply as possible three times at a leisurely rate. Until your lungs are completely full, then exhale the same, slowly, very slowly. Close your eyes and relax your whole body, don't make it hard, leave it soft. You still feel a little disturbed in your mind, don't you? now what you will do is breathe normally without concentrating on your breathing, but you will begin to concentrate on your mind, just try not to fight with your thought or thoughts that arise. For example, if a thought such as orange questions you, what are you? Question your answer, don't answer just question it, every thought that arises and your answer question it, however simple and silly it may seem to you. At least do it for 8 minutes. If a thought arises, for example: I feel ugly, I feel fat, I feel sad, I feel afraid, question them and your answer the same, every answer and question question it. This exercise is an effective technique and will help you quickly relax your mind, helping to modify your anxious thinking and channel it into basic thoughts, as those that do not make you feel anxious are known, and that little by little you learn to control and stop think about main thoughts that are the ones that cause anxiety to a lesser or greater extent.

Techniques for panic attacks

At this point, surely you already know all the discomfort and sensations that occur when you get one or before one manifests itself. When you realize that you have already passed the barrier of no return and you realize that one is going to give you, in those last seconds or as soon as the panic attack begins, manifesting itself with strong tremors, strong tachycardia, sweating, and excruciating fear, you feel that you are short of breath that you cannot expand your lungs that you want to scream, run away or perhaps you feel that your death is imminent. In order for your mind to react, it has to learn a signal, that is, so that your reactions are on time, and when you do it in those seconds you are able to start doing the following technique to contain the attack. Suppose you've been in a panic attack for seconds, the signal that you will give your mind to start lowering it can be different, a small slap or I recommend a strong pinch in your left hand. Once you perceive that signal, your mind will be aware that at that moment you will start doing the exercise, even though you feel terrible at those moments, the first thing you will do is:

- Cover your nose and mouth with both hands, do it with enough force so that you cannot breathe. You will do this despite the fact that in a panic attack you feel your breathing heavy and oppressed chest and shortness of breath. You will not breathe for 30 seconds, if you resist you will be depriving your central nervous system of the food that it will be supplying to the panic attack and therefore the entire flow of symptoms that you feel will immediately begin to drop, and this is because the nervous system will detect passing the 30 seconds of a drop in oxygen and it will activate your survival by giving it priorities, so the panic attack will immediately disappear. It is an excellent technique because you trick your nervous system directly responsible for a panic attack.

Once the 30 seconds have elapsed, you will take three breaths of air and again close your nose and mouth with all your might, this time for only 20 seconds. At that moment when your panic attack has gone down noticeably, you will tell yourself a positive affirmation that combined with the technique described will gradually make a positive mental pattern in each panic attack to the point where little by little you will begin to send the message to your subconscious and you will be more aware that once the panic attack passes you will send a message to your subconscious that it will not hurt you and there is no reason to fear. Therefore, although they will not be removed overnight, every time you have one you will know how to act and after having one, you will have a positive attitude and a better attitude, and this will fill your subconscious mind little by little with positive messages in reference to panic attacks, making a mental pattern, to the point that when you least expect it, after months of practice little by little they will begin to diminish and lose strength to the point of that one day they will disappear completely. This technique is scientifically supported in brain wave studies with computerized studies in panic attack patients.

Once all the panic symptoms have decreased thanks to oxygen deprivation to your brain for 30 seconds, you will repeat positive acceptance phrases such as: "Nothing bad happened to me because of the panic attack, the tremors and the tachycardia did not let me." no sequel because they are part of the anxiety and not of any organic disease that my mind believes I have. Nothing will happen to me, I will not die because I am completely healthy, it is only my mind that alerts me to change my negative mentality.

Self-convincing and accepting statements such as: It is not dangerous to have panic attacks, nothing will happen to me, I like to feel panic attacks, it feels good, I hope they hit me every day, self-deception statements of this type help greatly to confuse our subconscious and instead of generating what is expected, they generate the opposite; instead of appearing stronger they become weaker and weaker because an already expected routine does it and because you become familiar with the symptoms. And suddenly if it hits again they become weaker and no longer have the same strength. I took this thing that I mention for a month and wow! that at the beginning I was not completely convinced because they are simple accepting phrases, but incredibly the attacks began to lose strength within the first 3 weeks. Believe me,

It is very difficult to know and anticipate when a panic attack will arrive, but if it were to happen to you at home, I want a person close to you to be with you at all times. Suppose right now you are having a panic attack, by now you are covering your nose and mouth just as I specified above and this is to decrease your oxygen to your brain. Within 35 seconds your symptoms will begin to progressively decrease if you do not remove your hand from your mouth and nose. At this point you already feel controlled because you feel that they are diminishing, just like the fear that you felt in your mind, they begin to defend... your family member or person close to you with a firm voice, but without actually yelling at you, he will mention your name to remind you to mention at that moment some of the learned self-affirmation phrases that are to deceive your subconscious. For example: "I love the symptoms I feel when I have a panic attack every day, it feels great! subconscious have them give me every day ". Repeat these phrases over and over again, they can not only be affirmations but also affirmations wanting to give an active message to your subconscious. For example, reverse psychology to your unconscious works this way: "I love the tremors I feel, it's fun to feel the cold sensation, I really want more. I feel that feeling of lack of air, I like it, and phrases like that". it feels great! subconscious have them give me every day ". Repeat these phrases over and over again, they can not only be affirmations but also affirmations wanting to give an active message to your subconscious. For example, reverse psychology to your unconscious works this way: "I love the tremors I feel, it's fun to feel the cold sensation, I really want more. I feel that feeling of lack of air, I like it, and phrases like that". it feels great! subconscious have them give me every day ". Repeat these phrases over and over again, they can not only be affirmations but also affirmations wanting to give an active message to your subconscious. For example, reverse psychology to your unconscious works this way: "I love the tremors I feel, it's fun to feel the cold sensation, I really want more. I feel that feeling of lack of air, I like it, and phrases like that". I really want more. I feel that feeling of lack of air, I like it, and phrases like that". I really want more. I feel that feeling of lack of air, I like it, and phrases like that".

Positive phrases can be such as: "look anxiety! The panic attack didn't do anything to me, I'm alive so why be afraid if I already know what it feels like, nothing will happen to me, so I don't care if they give me the whole day, absolutely nothing will happen to me, never I will die of one. I want to be emphatic, no one dies of a panic attack despite the fact that in the first instance they are usually a disturbing, even terrifying experience. I assure you that yes, little by little you do this and you are disciplined and constant, you will begin to lose your fear until you become a routine and make them disappear in your mind. So at this point ask yourself why should I live in fear of a panic attack if nothing ever happens to anyone? So tell yourself, "This is personal. but I will not fear the next time or get paranoid (or) thinking that I am about to die because in truth a panic attack will never kill me. I will make it my friend and suddenly it will be gone, never to return. It is vital to have faith, and that the technique you do really works, and to practice them every day when you get up and when you go to bed. If you are disciplined and do not give way to laziness and discouragement, in a month you will begin to see results, and you will be surprised.

The habanero pepper method

Although this method is a bit energetic, it has been carried out less than 5 years ago in some of the best specialized centers around the world, as a rapid method for panic attacks. Its effectiveness has already been proven in real trials in some universities around the world. Although it is something drastic, but when the person who is experiencing it is in an attack, he feels that he is going to die due to the whole set of symptoms. When the symptomatology is triggered in an individual with this disorder, they know - they recognize the symptoms, but they are unable to stop it by force of will. However, with this method the process is quick to stop. Although, I do not recommend it for everyone due to the itchiness. If you are tolerant, I always recommend taking a bottle of water with you and a red or green habanero pepper. It reads pretty geeky, but drastic measures for drastic symptoms. In addition, personally I have verified the effectiveness in many of my patients, in a range of 79% it stopped them in the course of the attack.

When you identify the first symptoms, such as the sensation of imminent death or strong palpitations, which is the preamble to starting a strong panic attack, it is that fear of imminent danger, and that sometimes makes us act by impulsively running outside or to start shaking frantically. From the moment you identify that you are going to get one or that's it, at that moment you have to take out the habanero pepper and bite it all, yes, be careful! You shouldn't swallow it, just chew it and resist as long as you can: 1, 2, 3,4,5,6,7,8,9,10... seconds. You must feel the explosion of heat and burn like fire in your mouth for it to start to take effect.

Many people scratch themselves in panic attacks and somehow it comforts them to resist, but many times the brain does not react and continues immersed in an attack. But with a habanero chili you will react and you will begin to focus attention on reducing the symptoms because it will detect that the tongue is burning produced by capsaicin, which is what our brain detects as itching and fire, which is the active ingredient of the chili. In that moment that it detects that, it will prioritize that something is happening and therefore it will begin to rapidly reduce the symptoms of the panic attack, giving priority to that burning sensation in the mouth, and therefore it will stop the panic attack in a matter of two minutes. .

Before the attack reaches its highest point, the power of the habanero pepper will decrease all the symptoms coming from our brain, at this point it is time to start drinking plenty of water due to the sensation of fire in the mouth. This method is simple, but the side effect is extreme itching, but it's nothing you can't stand.

Technique for insomnia - falling asleep fast:
At this point you are quiet in your room ready to sleep, relaxed. Right now you turn off the lights and lie peacefully on your bed. Prior to this you have not eaten any heavy food. You left your cell phone downstairs or it's turned off. You also did not consume any sugar in the two hours before you fell asleep. And now you close your eyes because you are about to sleep.... Most likely, your thoughts gradually begin to activate as they do every night, and for this reason they prevent you from falling asleep quickly as you would like or your insomnia will not let you. Well, the first thing you will have to do before starting is to breathe from

your lying position with your eyes closed. Breathe in as deeply as possible and you will exhale as slowly as possible. This will make the muscles in the chest and neck area that you probably have tense due to the fear and trauma of knowing that you will not be able to sleep, activate everything unconsciously causing stress and anxiety. Once you do this for about 3 minutes and you have reached a slight relaxation, you will begin to make your mind free of thoughts, not blank, but try not to think about anything. Now you will start with the technique in total darkness.

With your eyes closed... at this precise moment in total darkness you will imagine that you are going in a zigzag if you read the zigzag correctly in your thoughts head-on in the dark. You will start moving forward with your zigzag thinking head on, obviously not imagining or thinking about your physical body with your mind alone, and the feeling or thought of zigzag... try to imagine the zigzag movement in your mind, don't move your eyes zigzag but your mind... after a few seconds you will perceive or notice that your mind will begin to get bored, at that moment you should not give room to any thought other than what you are doing; zigzagging ahead in the dark. After doing the first thing for a couple of minutes zigzagging straight ahead, you will suddenly imagine that you are falling downward into the void... I remind you, your mind is like the infinite universe, there is neither right nor left nor height, but in this exercise you will imagine direction in that darkness. I remind you, when your mind gets bored of falling into the void, you come back, that is, first you will zigzag in the dark (in the front line), but when you get bored, then you will imagine that you are falling into the void and when you get bored, go back. one side and then turn to the left side, and when you get bored again go up and then start all over again... you will soon realize that your mind will quickly get bored doing the directions, and that is why this technique is called redirections mental cognitive because it prevents your thoughts from focusing on those negative thoughts at the moment, and they only follow those channeled brain waves of thought like going zigzag in directions to the point that from so much falling into points of boredom the mind enters sleep states at any moment and you fall asleep, it is extremely effective. Since I no longer suffer from insomnia, I still use it when I have conferences and I need to fall asleep quickly, because in a matter of minutes I fall asleep. Obviously, to give this technique extra strength, I am leaving you with a list of the best infusions on the planet that help to channel sleep naturally, and that you can also combine with each other. All of them in themselves have relaxing and sedative properties that act directly on our nervous system, stimulating and quickly causing us to fall asleep. Besides insomnia, most work for general anxiety.

The best combined infusions against insomnia:
Valerian and kava tea
Kava with passion flower
lavender with valerian
Chamomile with lemon balm
Lemon leaves with Luisa herb
lemon balm with lavender tea
Ashwagandha with linden tea
Mint tea with licorice root
Passionflower with hops
tarragon with sage
rosemary with orange blossom
Passionflower with hops
Tarragon with linden tea
Consume a lot of omega 3 - fatty acids
Consume B complex
Sunbathe

Reprogram your subconscious mind and eliminate anxiety forever

As its name says, this mental technique resides mainly in reprogramming the mental patterns of your subconscious in a natural way so that you recover your normal state as before.

Most likely at this point you have already heard at some point about what is the subconscious or unconscious, and if so, it is likely that it will be easier for you to assimilate and understand everything. A large percentage of people have an erroneous or confused idea, they believe that the subconscious is a kind of locked room, where there are colossal amounts of recorded information to which we never usually have access. They also believe that this is the place where all the traumas, fears, habits, fears, and negative thoughts and everything from our childhood are stored. Bad or good situations that we no longer want to remember, etc. While there is some truth in all this, the truth is that the level of complexity of our subconscious is much more complex in reality. In this section we will deal a little bit in depth with our unconscious, and about the technique that I use to reprogram our subconscious in order to eliminate or control anxiety. From more than 6 thousand patients that I have treated directly in several decades, I can proudly say that this technique has a 93% effectiveness rate. The results are incredible if it is combined with all the techniques of the principle. Fortunately, our subconscious has the ability to be reprogrammed and once it is done, the before and after change in the mental health of the person involved is incredible. The vast majority of people think that it is not possible to eliminate anxiety through reprogramming, but it is because they have no idea of the wonderful power of our mind.

What is really our subconscious or unconscious mind?

Our unconscious is that area of our mind to which we do not have conscious entry or access. But this does not mean that we are not capable of doing it. What happens is that, from a conscious state, for example, when we analyze a task we only have access to an area of our conscious mind and the use of that area is what we use for some specific mental processes. Although, we always have that much more mysterious and powerful hidden part called the unconscious.

To make it clear, our conscious mind is all of our rational and analytical part that we have and it is the one that is always directly bombarded by all kinds of stimuli directly and indirectly and this is due to the senses that we have. But this great flow of information called stimuli is brutal, which is why it would be impossible for our conscious mind, that is, our (interior self) to process in such a short time, adding to the fact that much of the information that enters is unhelpful information. For this, our mind that is in charge of processing important data and not in our mind the one in charge, but rather it is our reticular system that is a type of filter in our brain that our mind has to automatically alert us, notify us that something is worth eliminating or No. To cite an example, If you are a fan of contact sports, perhaps your reticular system (sar) will automatically alert you that you have a certain inclination for information from the outside that is related to the sports universe. Contrary to an individual who is not interested in sports, his (sar) is most likely to overlook all that wealth of sports stimuli. According to some neuroscientific research in recent years, it indicates that our wonderful brain has the capacity to process approximately four hundred and thirty billion bits, however, we are only aware of about 20 thousand per second, excluding the rest solely by our subconscious mind. and discarding them afterwards. As additional information, They knew that we are only aware of 17% of the information that enters us through the senses, leaving 85% somehow stored directly in our unconscious mind. And it is precisely in that part of our mind where we store all our memories, good or bad habits that we have, customs, hobbies, tastes and a long etc. However, it is not only in charge of this, but our unconscious is in charge of the automatic execution of all the vast majority of our body's automatic biological tasks, such as extremely complex processes at the cellular level, such as making sure that our heart continues to beat while we sleep. , that our kidneys, liver, and other organs continue to function correctly, that our cells replicate and a long etc.

The way in which our unconscious reprograms itself through all the experiences we have had.

We have to be clear that our subconscious or unconscious mind does not think, that is, it does not analyze. Even without that, as you read above, it is capable of executing a colossal task of processes automatically at impressive speeds, adding that it manages all our processes of memories, habits, etc. So reading this you might be wondering, well, what? How come you don't think or analyze? Well, let's not forget that the rational analytical-logical part that is responsible for doing that is our conscious mind, that is, your inner self. And in our conscious it is the one that is in charge of carrying out all that chain of logical processes. The conscious mind (inner self) upon receiving hundreds of stimuli in the form of information, what it does is process it, then analyze and label it. Contrary to that, What our unconscious mind does is receive all the information from the outside as true, that is, all kinds of real or unreal thoughts take them as true. Let's cite an example, if I receive information from abroad, let's say I look at a black dog, my conscious mind interprets it, then analyzes it and labels it all in a matter of microseconds, once labeled it sends it directly to the subconscious. When my subconscious receives it, it will not ask, it will not think, it will only receive it, it will say thank you and it will process it, it will file it for future use if my self needs it. To understand let's make a better analogy. Suppose your conscious mind is a train pilot, and your subconscious mind is the train. As you can see, the powerful train-engine without the pilot would do nothing, but obeys the driver according to the orders he gives him. He does not question, he does not complain, he does not think, he does not analyze, he only receives orders from his pilot and complies with them.

The power that dwells in our powerful subconscious mind

As we have already learned, we already know what role our unconscious plays in our lives. Not only is it responsible for all the automatic processes that keep us alive, but it also manages our memories, habits, etc. We have already said that from our conscious mind we hardly use a part of our mind, and it is because we only need it to carry out a rigorous task that we execute. However, there are hundreds of tasks that are important to our lives, but we carry them out automatically without analyzing or "thinking" and this is due to the fact that our habits, practices, vices, are stored in that area of our unconscious. memories.

To make it easier to understand, driving a car. When we just start driving classes to have skill at first it is difficult – confusing, you almost crash, you cannot have coordination in looking forward and behind etc. And it was almost complicated for all of us, right? because not only do we have to look straight ahead, but we must also constantly pay attention to the rear-view mirrors, adding that we must control the speed, the brake, the gearbox and many more factors. Adding to that if the car is standard an extra problem is. However, as time goes by and we become right-handed at the wheel, there comes a time when we all do it quickly and automatically, without thinking about it. And it does not mean that by doing it automatically without analyzing it we are not aware but imagine what danger we would have. What happens is that the mysterious and complex mechanism of all our habits in our unconscious facilitates the whole process without being almost aware that we are doing it. So at that point conscious processes are no longer needed where you involve your conscious mind, that is, the execution of meticulous and rigorous analyzes to make sure of the task in question, for example, how much force you give to the brake or accelerator, etc. At this point you may ask, but by doing that doesn't it mean that I am aware? well yes, but what happens is that when you press the accelerator or the brake they have different touches and if you pressed differently or vice versa it would feel very different and at that moment the habit gear of your subconscious that you have saved would come into play and you would immediately press the correct one . impressive don't you think?

So here comes what matters to us, how do I program my subconscious mind?

So, if our unconscious does not think or analyze, or ask what it receives from the outside, how the hell does it know what it should and has to do? Well, at this point it uses customs or habits - practices, not so much biological processes to keep us alive.

However, what interests us at the moment... let's look at the other functions of our subconscious mind in our life. In our unconscious there are hundreds and hundreds of good and bad habits that we have assimilated throughout our existence and based on experiences. Many of them are essential and positive while others are harmful and negative, for example, good habits such as drinking water, eating, exercising, etc. Contrary to the harmful ones like smoking, stealing, thinking negatively and a long etc.

As we already mentioned, the unconscious mind receives everything from our inner self, that is, the unconscious does not analyze or question, it only receives it. And he says "it's okay to send them to me, I'll file them for when you use it." Therefore, our unconscious is formed by a set of thoughts, mental thought patterns based on information sent from the conscious.

Something very important at this point is that we see two elements, that the subconscious is highly vulnerable to self-programming before or through situations of traumatic emotional impacts, such as rape, torture, kidnapping, violence, etc. When the subconscious has been exposed to disturbing situations, it usually changes its mental patterns, creating trauma to a lesser or greater extent for what it experienced.

The second element of self reprogramming is the repetition of negative thoughts that one regularly repeats to oneself or, wow! assimilating from the outside of bad or good companies or throughout experiences. To cite an example, if you suffered sexual abuse or violence, it is likely that if you did not receive timely help that when you grow up you may do that to other people or channel that trauma through violence or anxiety. Others are the repetitions of thoughts that are given in this way. Suppose we consciously think and repeat to ourselves: "I'm scared, I'm a failure, why do I exercise, I can't lose weight, I'm afraid to go to... anxiety can't be cured...", as we pilots of the great thinking machinery of this class, What do you think will happen if we think like this? that you will never overcome anxiety, that you will not lose weight, you will be a failure with all due respect, and very faithful to what you (conscious) think, your subconscious mind will obey faithfully because you are sending orders, and it will put obstacles for you to do not achieve any goal, and these come as if you say: "I will never heal from anxiety", then when repetitive negative thoughts of this nature occur at a certain moment, you must do the opposite, although by nature we do not want to and be an extra waste of energy. Although your subconscious wanted to send the answer and doubts appear, you should not pay attention, but rather you should respond with contrary thoughts, even though, as I mentioned, you absolutely do not want to fight with yourself. And therein lies the magic of all this,

There is a phrase that I love from George Lucas that says:"As much as you think you can or if you think you can't, in both you are right."You know that the big difference between a person who succeeds and a person who doesn't, is only one thing, and that is what they think of themselves. And so true is the hackneyed saying that "belief is power", and it is totally true. As rational individuals when we are time after time for many months or years bombarding our minds with all kinds of harmful, limiting, poor negative thoughts, such as: "I am useless, I am useless, nobody will love me, I am useless for this, I can't do this because, I'm worthless, I want to kill myself, I'm ugly, I'm fat, etc".

Maybe it's not entirely your fault, but rather your indirect experiences when you were little, but luckily it's time to get down to business. Although there are also people who have recorded in their unconscious those patterns and habits that have led them to success and free from anxiety and with high self-esteem since they were little. There are both sides of the coin. At this moment you may be wondering, you who are suffering or who want to give this book to help a family member or friend, is it really possible to do it in a short time? Well, I answer you, of course it is possible! and it is precisely what we will see next.

Before moving on to the next chapter, I want you to keep in mind a very important aspect of why the vast majority are not successful when they want to eliminate or control anxiety from their lives. Just as you were programming your unconscious without thinking over time, now that you suffer from generalized anxiety due to direct or indirect causes and you suffer from this disease, and now that you find out how to reprogram it, you are ready to do it, the time comes when you get frustrated and you stop because you want to do it from one day to the next, and believe me, it doesn't work like that. In order to eliminate it, you need logical time so that your mind is programmed to healthy habits, positive thoughts, and therefore, you must be disciplined and not desperately looking at your goal in the future with mental firmness. I do not want to say that it will take you years to achieve your goal and banish anxiety, no! but if you put discipline on your part, I can assure you that it will be months with the techniques that you will learn below. It's like everything, the peasant first clears the land in which he sows the seed, then he waters it and at the end of his hard work he harvests. Have faith in what I tell you, because every day I see patients cured with this system after several months immersed in the method.

Essential techniques for reprogramming your unconscious usingpositive affirmations

We will use the first technique known as positive thought patterns, which we will use to reprogram our mind every day by repeating them daily until we believe them and then change our behavior.

As previously mentioned, the unconscious tends to be very susceptible to daily repetitive thought patterns for a long time. To cite a practical example, if you repeat positive thoughts to yourself daily such as; "I have the ability to achieve what I set out to do, I am capable of doing... I love myself, I have a lot of courage because I am unique, I will overcome anxiety because I will change my mind, I will act differently positive, I will change all my negative habits into positive ones both mentally and practically etc.". All the changes of thoughts that are waiting deep in your unconscious will gradually diminish in our inner heart and the old ones will go away, being displaced by new ones to the point that they will remain more and more in the background, and when you least think they will leave forever and will lose strength in your behavior of acting, making you not to have those negative inclinations to behave in reality. And it will have an impact on your life by gradually leaving anxiety and all its derivative disorders that you have whether panic attacks, social phobia etc.. Real positive phrases that you think change your thinking with repetition and with your action like: "I can do it, I am able to do it, I will do it, I will do it, I will achieve everything I propose, I will not let myself be discouraged no matter if my day is negative or positive in results, I will continue to overcome anxiety thinking positive and realistic".

All this kind of positive suggestive thoughts, what they do is to encourage us and to give us encouragement of instructions thought about ourselves in the most recondite of our mind to execute in the future making as main rule to change our conduct gradually, the old for the new day after day, week after week, month after month until arriving at a level where that inner power of the subconscious enters in action and makes change everything in our person. It is something more complex to explain in lines, but it happens.

When these unhealthy, harassing negative thoughts appear, what you will do is to introduce any positive thought, but that is as short as possible, and that serves to replace that intrusive thought. Let's do something practical, let's suppose you are lying in your bed and suddenly a series of catastrophic thoughts begin to appear such as 'you could die or whatever you can think of', then what you will do is to think of something positive and believe them as: "I am beautiful, I am worth a lot, I will achieve this at any cost, etc.. In this way what you will do is that those negative routine thought patterns will gradually become shorter and shorter until they no longer exist in your unconscious or it will be easier to eliminate them when they arise.

Our powerful mind is capable of doing anything you believe. Now that you know that it is possible, I am sure you want to try to do it or not, but please, if you try it, try to do it with patience and calm so you do not despair and do not end up abandoning the method. What matters to you now is your generalized anxiety and from there you will go on to the derived disorders. So, this is what you will do, from the time you wake up until you go to sleep, I want you to repeat in your mind either spoken or in mental voice positive affirmations, no matter what they are, but they must be positive so that you go pouring more and more positivism to your unconscious and go replacing the old behaviors and mental patterns, and in addition go away your anxiety from your life that is as mentioned above, those thoughts, bad memories or moments have been the triggers of the disorder.

So, repeat each affirmation 27 times seven times and move on to the next one that you believe will help you. But I want you to have faith, not just parrot them. I want you to really believe them, that way your unconscious mind will record them as a real and capable mental pattern. This is not a bunch of self-help information as it abounds nowadays, no, on the contrary, it has been proven by neuroscience and verified with thousands of patients I have treated. A large percentage tends to despair because they want to see changes from one day to the next, but unfortunately things in our reality do not work like in the movies, but happen gradually, similar to the fruit of an apple tree. From the time the soil was prepared to sow the seed until the fruit is harvested. The idea is hour after hour, day, week, month after month to weaken all those negative habits until we break them and replace them with new positive habits in practice and in our thinking. And this can be achieved with any trait of your personality that you think is negative. For example, if you want to eliminate smoking, that is, every day 70 times you should repeat to yourself every morning and evening: "I will stop smoking", that thought in your subconscious will be translated "I want to stop smoking", and in practice you have to make an effort to obey it, and in that way your subconscious will do the rest. If at the beginning of the first week you achieve something in the struggle, little by little it will become easier, to the point that several months later, regardless of relapses, you will have succeeded. The power of this method is that anything can be accomplished, and with anxiety it is the same.

"I'm going to beat anxiety", repeat it 1000 times, but you will accompany it with real activities not just mental ones. You will exercise, think positively, socialize if you have social phobia etc. I want you to be aware that everything is in your mind, and you already have the tools to start and be able to eliminate it from your life. And if you feel able to go to a specialist if you decide to do so. If my patients and I achieved it following the same combined method, I know you will be able to do it.

Reprogram your unconscious with the so-called alpha waves

This technique basically resides in entering a deep state of relaxation. Once you breathe in slowly and exhale in a controlled manner, you will choose any technique from the previous chapters. The positive affirmations of this technique basically consist of those of the previous exercise, with the difference that when we are executing them we will be in a state of relaxation called alpha, so the process will be much faster. It is already fully demonstrated that our brain emits electrical impulses when it receives information from outside, and these impulses are then transmitted to each other through a large central neural network. All these incessant impulses that are given through the entire neural network produce small rhythmic movements of waves that are scientifically known as brain waves. To sum it up, we have four main waves in our mind, which are: delta, beta, alpha and theta. And each one usually has to do with different behaviors or activities in human beings, let's see each one in summary.

In alpha waves: They appear when our brain enters into processes of low activity, such as states of relaxation and happiness. In resonances they appear as slow rhythmic waves. They appear when, for example, you are walking relaxed near the sea, under the forest, listening to those waves of the sea, birds singing, beautiful melodies, we have sex, we love, like when practicing yoga, in short, they appear in all those activities of pleasure and happiness.

beta waves: these waves are almost always active, and that is when our brain is in normal mode. Like when we are awake looking out the window... it becomes more active when we begin to carry out processes where certain analysis is required, such as when we are going to do something with our hands, mathematical problems, going down stairs, etc.

Theta waves: This kind of waves appear when we are sleeping and in each of the sleep phases. They are also achieved in practices such as yoga, mindfulness, meditation, and deep breathing states.

Delta waves: these appear when we are in very deep dreams. Analyzing the four waves, surely you already realized that the best state to reprogram our subconscious mind is the alpha mental state for obvious reasons, because we are conscious, but in a state of deep relaxation, and most of the techniques shown in this section are for use in this state. The quieter and calmer you are is when your unconscious will be more receptive to introducing suggestible positive affirmations. Repeat them until exhaustion, but with faith, at least 15 minutes or 20 or an hour in the morning and afternoon, the idea is not to get bored doing them, that's why 15 is fine, but it depends on each person, if you want quick results, it will be more and more practice. Remember that every time you tell yourself a positive affirmation, answer yourself with a Why? For example, "I will be cured of anxiety", why? -Because I will do each of the techniques until I get out of my anxious state, I will achieve this dream because I will fight until I achieve it, I will lose weight because I will exercise etc." The important thing here is that there is an emotion involved and that there is a certain emotional impact, I will heal, I will heal from anxiety because I value myself, because I want to fulfill my dreams without seeing myself disabled by this, I want to be a lawyer, I want to be an athlete and travel the world, I want to get married etc. All this combination of emotions - responses together give better results because it has a main objective and is not just repeating the affirmation, such as saying, "I will lose weight, If you say it like that, they don't have that extra emotion on the contrary. If you say it with the affirmation and then with the emotion of why you will do it, "I will lose weight", why? because I want to have a girlfriend, I don't want to get sick, I want to look pretty, I want to fulfill my dreams, etc. Everything together creates a stronger emotion and drives to act to achieve that goal. Thus, therefore, your unconscious will strive to achieve said goal until it is achieved.

Conclusion

With the endorsement of neuroscience and being accredited as one of the most respected specialists against anxiety by different important magazines in the world, I am an eyewitness of every day seeing the effectiveness of all this combined system, obviously it is not the same to read it and apply it from a book than doing it with me, but it starts with something. We have a great friend in our unconscious, as well as an enemy if we neglect him with unhealthy habits and thoughts, therefore, he reacts with anxieties, disorders and illnesses. Luckily, you now know how to reprogram it. It's easy, just follow the above. Just have discipline, faith and you will heal. Five months is realistic to have some real impact on your unconscious and give a big change to your life.

Do not forget to leave me a sincere comment and how was your experience and results after having carried them out. Thank you very much and I wish you wholeheartedly well, your friend:

Dr Albert Jhonson

Synthesized book of the real method used in person by Dr. Albert Jhonson to treat anxiety and its disorders